FUN
PROJECTS
FOR HANDS-ON
CHARACTER
BUILDING

RICK & MARILYN BOYER

Homeschool Press

FUN PROJECTS FOR
HANDS-ON CHARACTER BUILDING

©1996 by Rick and Marilyn Boyer

Cover design by Mark Dinsmore

Book design by Brian Michael Taylor, 2Cor3:3

ISBN 0-9645396-5-9

Published by Homeschool Press
229 S. Bridge Street
PO Box 254
Elkton MD 21922-0254

Send requests for information to the above adress.

Printed in the United States of America

"And you shall..."

*And you shall
love the LORD your God
with all your heart
and with all your soul
and with all your might.
And these words, which I am
commanding you today
shall be on your heart...*

—DEUTERONOMY 6:5–6 NASB

2

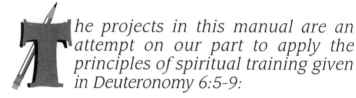

he projects in this manual are an attempt on our part to apply the principles of spiritual training given in Deuteronomy 6:5-9:

And you shall love the Lord your God with all your heart and with all your soul and with all your might. And these words, which I am commanding you today, shall be on your heart; and you shall teach them diligently to your sons and shall talk of them when you sit in your house and when you walk by the way and when you lie down and when you rise up. And you shall bind them as a sign on your hand and they shall be as frontals on your forehead. And you shall write them on the doorposts of your house and on your gates. (NASB)

First we are commanded to "teach them diligently" to our children. Then we are given some specific principles by which to do it. We are to "talk of them" at specific times. "When you sit in your house" (at meals or in leisure time), "when you walk by the way" (traveling from place to place), "when you lie down" (bedtime), and "when you rise up" (first thing in the morning).

3

Then we are told some specific ways to communicate God's truths: We are to "bind them as a sign upon your hand and they shall be as frontal on your forehead." That means Scripture should be part of our wearing apparel. "And you shall write them on the doorpost of your house and on your gates." So Scripture should be a part of the physical environment of our homes as well.

When we put a Bible verse on a child's sweatshirt with fabric crayon, he is reminded of the presence of God by his wearing apparel. When we have Scripture plaques on the walls we get the benefits of God's Word on the doorpost and gates. When bedrooms contain character quality quilts and Bible story curtains the child is reminded of the Lord when he lies down and when he rises up. Car games can be used on trips to work Scripture into the child's conversation when he "walks by the way." As for when he sits in his house...well, sometimes it seems kids never just sit. So Scripture plates, cups, and tablecloths can be used at mealtimes when, hopefully, they will be still for a few minutes at least.

4

You can see that what we are trying to do here is give you some ideas by which you can saturate your child's home environment with God's Word. All responsible Christian parents have a deep desire to train their children up in the nurture and admonition of the Lord, but most of us were not brought up in the kind of home we hope to provide for our own families, and we need a little direction as to how to go about the job. The projects in this manual are mostly original; some are borrowed from other parents and some are adapted from methods by which other things than spiritual truth are taught. They are mostly simple things that we have found to be helpful to our family and it is our sincere hope that some of them will be useful to you.

Nobody in the world has a more important job than a Christian parent. May God bless you as you apply yourself to the task.

–Rick and Marylin Boyer

Section 1
Building Obedience

*Let every person
be in subjection
to the governing authorities.
For there is no authority
except from God,
and those which exist
are established by God.*

—ROMANS 13:1 *NASB*

8

OD HAS ORDAINED that our lives should operate according to orderly rules and principles.

One of these principles states that in all of life there are certain human authorities through which God makes His will known to us. These human agents are not authorized to violate God's will in exerting control, their right to hold a place of leadership depends upon their righteous behavior. Those under authority have no right to rebel against God's ordained authorities. The only time in which obedience is not required is that case in which a human power requires one to do something which would violate the will of a higher authority. Because all authority comes from God, every human authority—whether the king, the parent, or the pastor—must submit to the rule of God in order to wield legitimate authority.

Because people often misuse their authority, it is easy to grow reluctant in our responses to some people. Often we lose sight of a ruler's position in reaction to negative

aspects of his personality. In our day, it has become accepted and even fashionable to be "liberated" from the rulers whom God has put over us. This is tragic. Those authorities are there to protect us, to punish evil, and praise those who do well. The fact that leaders do not always fulfill their responsibilities does not provide us with justification to fail in our own.

Children need to be taught to obey. That means to obey God first, and under Him, all human authorities. While it is true that there may come times when a human authority must be disobeyed in order to obey God, these cases are few and far between. The vast majority of the rules and laws with which we live are clearly for our own good and the order and health of society. Speed limits, laws against murder and theft, etc., are all for the protection of the people. I want my children always to be willing to take a stand, however unpopular, and lay down their lives in defense of it if it is right in the eyes of God, but there is more to authority than discerning when God must be obeyed and man disobeyed. The crux of the matter is that God's will for us is that we have a heart of obedience. Scripture

10

contains abundant information, both in injunction and example, that shows the folly and wickedness of rebellion. We must learn to see God's hand behind the hard to live with idiosyncrasies of those in authority over us and realize a simple but obscure fact: We would never learn a true spirit of submission if it were always easy to obey. It is only by learning to live with people who, even though they are given the responsibility of wielding power, have the same human failings that we have, that we are tested and proved in regard to our obedience. If we cannot obey our human rulers when it is unpleasant to do so, how can God count on us to go the extra mile in His cause when the pressure is on?

God's plan is for our children to develop a heart of obedience at home in the early years. The comparatively gentle reproofs of the parent are sufficient to teach sons and daughters to have a responsive heart to God. If we parents fail, Psalm 27:10 comes into play: "When my father and my mother forsake me, then the LORD will take me up." (KJV) The sad thing about this is that if we fail to break the child's fleshly will at home, he will develop

11

calluses on it that God later will have to penetrate by the use of much stronger and more lasting reproofs. It is not unkind to break the will of a child lovingly. It is unkind to break it unlovingly, and perhaps worse to fail to break it at all.

The following pages give some ideas we have found useful in training our own children. They do not take the place of spankings, but will reduce the incidence of necessary reproofs by teaching children the spirit of obedience. Of course, there is no better teaching tool than a good example from the parent. We should remember that next time we are tempted to complain about how low the speed limit is.

Obedience Exercises
This is sort of a game, but it really has a serious effect on a child's obedience.

Explain to the kids that you have a challenge for them, and that if they do well they will get a treat. Go out in the yard if weather permits, or just do the project in the

house. Call out instructions for the children such as, "Lie down," "Stand up." Instruct them to "walk backward, walk forward, run forward, stop, turn left, hop on one foot," etc. Make it a challenge. Act as if you are enjoying it yourself, which is not difficult to do, because some of the results—when instructions come a little too fast or get confused—are really funny. To make it really special, have Dad do the exercises with the kids while Mom calls out the instructions. Give occasional surprises, such as calling for a sudden stop-and-lie-down in the middle of a dead run across the yard. Our kids always enjoy this game, and we spice it up—not with competition but by calling out lots of encouragement and challenges. It is often helpful to encourage a child to do a chore or errand he may not really like doing by calling on the same fun principle. For instance, "Nathan, I want you to take this towel down to the laundry room. Walk backwards all the way down and backup, and let's see if you can keep your left eye closed the whole time."

Training Sessions

One day back when we had only four children (seems like forever ago) Marilyn mentioned that she had endured a frustrating time in the supermarket that afternoon because the kids, who were all six and under, kept getting into things and doing things that distracted her from shopping. They were not being really bad or disobedient, but they did not seem to understand what was and was not appropriate behavior. I expect you can identify with that. Well, being a former police dog trainer, I diagnosed this as a situation requiring a training session. Since then, we have had many training sessions for different situations, and we have found them very helpful.

If it sounds as if I am suggesting you treat your kids like dogs, I am. You see, children share a few characteristics with dogs. Children, like dogs (and adults, for that matter) will do things for which they are rewarded and avoid doing things for which they are punished. A simple concept, but one that is apparently ignored or unknown by many

14

parents. Kids, like dogs, really want to obey because they want and need the approval of their parents. And kids, like dogs, are frustrated by improper training in how to please their parents.

By this I mean that we take the children to a place they may never have been before. or seldom have been before, and act as if we expect them to know exactly what behavior is appropriate—even though they have no previous experience or instruction to guide them. The problem, of course, is that we have failed to see the situation from the child's point of view. We assume that because we know how to act in this common situation, everybody knows how to act in this common situation, including children.

The fact is, if you have a good relationship with your children, they want to obey because it makes you happy with them and they need that. There is, of course, the sin nature still to be dealt with, and only the rod will cure some outbreaks of "willfulitis." But assuming that you have basic general control of your child, the biggest gap remaining in your relationship is probably instruction in how to behave in specific situations (and in unexpected situations, by observing general principles).

To train our children how to act in the supermarket, we at first were going about it all wrong. We took them to the store with no previous instruction, as if we expected them to know by instinct that they were to stay behind Mommy and the cart, stay to the side of the aisle, talk only in quiet voices, and of course keep their hands off all those fascinating things on the shelves. Our initial approach was to plunge right on into the store, march down the aisles, and reprove the kids after they had already done the wrong thing. The result was that most of the communication we had with the children was negative. There was not much opportunity for praising right behavior, the kids could not exhibit it because they did not know what it was, except that it was something other than the actions for which they already had been corrected. So the entire shopping trip, it seemed, was spent hearing about all the things they should not have done. Some fun.

16

We finally realized we were not being fair to the children. So we sat them down and had a little talk. We told them that we really appreciated their attempts to please us, and we were glad that they wanted to obey. We said that we loved them and wanted to help them to obey so they would be happy, obedience is the only way to happiness for children or adults. For that reason, we said, we were going to do a fun project. We were going to have a training session. Then we proceeded to explain that we were having a little problem in some places such as stores,because Mommy and Daddy had not let the kids know what they needed to do. We then told them what behavior we needed from them in the supermarket, and the next time Mommy and the boys went grocery shopping, Daddy went along to help with the training. Mommy went down the aisles with little Joshua in the cart baby seat, followed by the other three boys and Daddy bringing up the rear. As we went, I took every opportunity to praise the boys and encourage them by telling them that they were doing what we had instructed them to do. Occasionally, I had to make a correction, for which I would call ahead to Marilyn and stop the whole caravan while I explained—gently, I hope—what needed to be done differently. We were making the training a priority, with the shopping secondary. That naturally made the shopping trip longer than usual, but having anticipated this it was no big irritation. We would remind you that this kind of training is not to be done on a trip that must be hurried, or it will result in frustration for the parents and hurt for the children. When children are made to feel that the parents expect perfect behavior in pressured circumstances, they will give up on pleasing you and cease trying, except as they are forced to.

In conducting a training session, there are a number of things to bear in mind. First give plenty of verbal instruction in advance. Make the rules few, clear and simple. Second. make the training the priority of the trip and do not worry about accomplishing everything else you normally would at the place, wherever it is. Third, take adequate time for each step of training. Hurried instructions are often confusing instructions. Hurried corrections are often harsh corrections. Fourth,

18

involve both parents when possible. Fifth, be prepared to repeat the training session. The more demanding the behavior required, the longer the duration of the trip or activity, the younger the children and/or the more complicated the instructions, the more training will be required.

For what situations will your children need special training? Some possibilities are stores, churches, restaurants, cars, a friend's house, outdoors at home, indoors at home (eg. we have " indoor voices" and no running), and on field trips. We have more need for training sessions than some parents, because we have more children. One or two children usually do not require the repetition of instructions that six or seven children do, so some things that require special training trips for our family would not for yours.

Do training sessions really help? In our supermarket training, we did it on one Saturday only, I forget whether we went to only one or a couple of stores. But before the trip was over, we had heard comments from other shoppers on how well our children

were behaving. That continued on succeeding shopping trips, when Mommy was handling the boys alone.

Real-Life Character Stories

Scripture says that the testimony of the LORD is sure, making the simple person wise. One story we have told our children as a real-life testimony of the LORD is one about our former Sunday School teacher's son, David. When David was just a very small boy, he had crossed the street for some reason and was about to step into the street to come back home. His father, apparently just having realized that David was not where he had supposed, looked up and saw David about to walk out in front of a car. Dad shouted, "David, No" David stopped in his tracks as the car went whizzing by. Because David knew the meaning of the word "No" and obeyed without hesitation, he was alive and unhurt. Had he failed to obey and obey instantly, he likely would have been killed.

Such stories are very valuable. Our children love to hear about real events in the lives of real people, and if they know the person the story is about, so much the better. Perhaps the best character-lesson stories of all are the ones we tell them from our own life experiences. I have told them about the time I burned my face playing with firecracker powder, and almost lost my sight. I have told them about how my horse kicked me in the chest because of my own carelessness. Come to think of it, I have had quite a few mistakes to tell them stories about. Hopefully it will keep them from making the same mistakes. In regard to that idea, by the way, you may have heard someone say, as often I have, that the only way we learn the lessons of life is to make the mistakes ourselves. You just have to make your own mistakes, they say. You cannot learn from the lives of others. They are dead wrong, of course. I am sure there are some lessons we learn only from our own experience, but to say that we learn nothing from the experiences of others is to say that we are rather stupid. (I am always tempted to ask one of those learn-it-yourselfers if they think it is a bad idea to sleep on busy railroad tracks,

and whether they learned that lesson by experience.) This is a very good tool for teaching character and wisdom to your children in an interesting way. In fact, on those occasions when I am alone with my kids for a minute, such as when Mom is in the store and we are waiting in the car, the first thing that often happens is somebody begging, "Dad, tell us a story!"

If's

This is a fun and effective way to prepare the child for situations that probably will arise sooner or later.

Another form of story teaching is to create hypothetical situations and ask the child to deal with one in theory. It deals with certain situations in particular, but also ingrains themes and principles that are needed to deal with many other circumstances than just those discussed in the story. Examples: "Jimmy, if you were over at Johnnie's house playing and he said, 'Let's go in and watch TV,' what would you do?" "Rickey, if you were out in the woods and you saw a dog acting strangely as if it were sick, what would you do?" Sometimes the child will have a ready answer. Then is a good time to reaffirm this right idea in his mind and minister to his self-image by congratulating him and praising his thinking. Sometimes, the child will have an idea of what should be done in the hypothetical circumstance, but will gain further insight from some clarification. In that case, offer some little helps such as, "I wonder if there are any dog sicknesses that make dogs dangerous to people?" Rather than filling out the whole lesson for him, you are letting him exercise his own creativity by priming his mental pump and then letting him gush on. There is, of course, a place for simply telling your child exactly what he will and will not do: "Never get in a car with a stranger."

Obedience Book

Our oldest son, Rickey, had a mind of his own right from the start. I gave him his first corporal correction when he was eight or nine

months old, and it had an immediate positive effect. I remember that it was on a Sunday afternoon, and when we picked him up from the church nursery that evening, it was the first time he reached out for Daddy instead of Mommy, as he always had previously. Rickey was a very active, ambitious, aggressive (not violent—just enthusiastic) boy. He was interested in everything and into everything. He seemed to get an unusually high number of spankings, but they seemed to be necessary. So Marilyn began looking for ways to teach obedience to Rickey aside from correction. One idea she came up with was Rickey's obedience book. Each page of the book had a stick-figure drawing illustrating a situation. This was accompanied by a Bible verse relating to the picture. Mom would then, at Rickey's daily special time, go through the notebook with him, and they would talk about each picture. One was a picture of Rickey getting a spanking, and written below the picture, Hebrews 12:11 in Phillips' version. Another was a picture of Ricky with Mommy and Daddy, and the caption was Proverbs 6:23, which Mom paraphrased to say, "For Daddy & Mommy's advice is a beam of light directed

24

into the dark corners of Rickey's mind, to warn Rickey and give Rickey a good life." Another was a picture of Rickey surrounded by other people looking at him. The caption was Proverbs 20:11, paraphrased by Mom to say, " The character of even Rickey can be known by the way he acts—whether what he does is pure and right."

Irritation List and Chart

Here is a project that will help you isolate what the problem is and design a way to meet the need.

When you are having one of those days when the kids are driving you bonkers but not really doing anything out-and-out disobedient. First, sit down and start a list of all the things, no matter how small, that the children have done today that bothered you. You may find in the process of doing this that you have simply been too touchy. If so, change yourself and not your children. If not, go ahead with your list. Then, hang on to the list for a day or two and add to it. The things you write will

25

mostly be insignificant in themselves; things that if they were not repeated you would scarcely notice. But added together, they can build up and build up until your children finally have the unsettling experience of seeing Mom or Dad go ballistic. Once you complete your list, make a chart to teach the children how to avoid doing things that bother you. We hung the chart we came up with in the classroom to help the kids remember. It was arranged in vertical columns:

Irritation	Insights into Quality Misused	Scripture to Remember	Project to Do
"Hey Mom!!" (Yelling to mom as soon as I step in the door)	Self-control (Wanting mom to talk to me immediately)	Proverbs 16:32 "He who is slow to anger is better than the mighty. And he who rules his spirit, than he who captures a city."	Walk quietly through the house and find Mommy then speak to her when she is ready.

26

Go through the chart with the children each day you are in the classroom, or as often as desperation drives you to it. This is one way you can deal with problems before they arise and avoid them, rather than having to feel that you are constantly reproving, criticizing, and correcting your children.

Scripture Obedience Songs

Several times during the past several years Marilyn has done a month-long unit on obedience. Part of her program for that part of the day was to sing a number of Scripture songs dealing with obedience. You can find songs to suit your purpose in a number of places, perhaps in some Sunday School material or on some of your children's music cassettes. There are books of songs intended for use in church programs for children, check your local Christian bookstore. This is also a good addition to your music class if you have one. Why just study music when you can also study the message of the songs?

Obedience Quiz

Give the child a question and a Bible verse to look up for the answer. For older boys and girls, let them use Strong's Concordance to find their own references. Some sample questions and answers:

? What was the result of Jesus' obedience to His parents? Lk. 2:52

? What does the Bible say disobedience is like? I Sam. 15:23

? What will you reap if you do not obey our authorities? Rom. 13:2

? In what things should you obey your parents? Col. 3:20

? What does God promise you if you honor your parents? Eph. 6:1-3

? What does the Bible say about a son who rejects his father's instruction? Prov. 15:5

? Where does all authority come from? Rom. 13:1

? What does the Bible call government leaders? Rom. 13:6,7

Section 1
Building Obedience

28

? What should your attitude be toward your church leaders? I Thess. 5:12,13

? What two ways should you respond to those in authority over you? Heb. 13:17

♦ True or False: Your spiritual authorities will one day give an account to God for the way in which they watched over your soul. Heb. 13:17

? If you obey your authorities, whom are you really obeying? Col. 3:24,25

? Should you obey an authority who has a wrong attitude? I Pet 2:18

? If you disobey your authorities, whose name suffers shame? 1 Tim.6:1

? What is bound up in your heart? Prov. 22:15

? What will drive rebellion away from you? Prov. 22:15

? Who is in control of your authorities? Prov. 21:1

? What will happen if you continue to stubbornly disobey? Prov. 29:1

? What did Jesus learn and what will we learn by rough things we suffer? Heb. 5:8

29

A reasonable question would be where in the world to get new quiz questions. The answer lies in your personal devotional time. We are all required to study God's Word. He may use the needs of your children to cue you in to an area He wants you to study for their benefit and your own. If you want to teach your children about obedience, take a Strong's Concordance and look up words such as obey, rule, authority, etc. You will find plenty of verses relating to the topic, and clues to other related words that also can be researched.

Section 2
Building A Pure Heart

*This book of the law shall not
depart from your mouth,
but you shall meditate on it
day and night,
so that you may be careful to do
according to all that is written in it;
for then you will make
your way prosperous,
and then you will have success.*

—JOSHUA 1:8 NASB

32

IN PSALM 1:3 we are promised that if we meditate on God's Word day and night we will be prosperous in everything that we do.

A similar promise is given in Joshua l:8. The Bible is replete with claims that those who fill their minds with the words and laws of God will make wise decisions and be people of great spiritual power. If we believe the Scriptures, it would behoove us to saturate ourselves with it much more.

The act of meditation has been described as "memorizing and digesting Scripture so that it becomes a living part of my life." This chapter contains some simple ways in which your children can internalize principles from the Word of God. We often say that the key to academic success is good spiritual health. Matthew 6:33 tells us to seek first God's kingdom and righteousness, and all we need of other things will be added to us. This is no less true in the area of learning than anywhere else. We have found that by using every opportunity to fill our childrens' minds with the truth of God, we build in them a

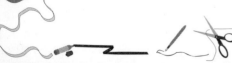

33

sensitivity to truth that we, their parents, cannot match. My eldest son once, at about eight or nine years of age, memorized five verses of Scripture in 35 minutes. That was on the same day I had spent two hours working on eight verses.

To program Scripture into your child's mind is to make him aware of and sensitive to the truth, build in him a distaste for that which is wicked or unworthy, and insulate him from the distraction of many emotional conflicts and worldly attractions. It is to free him to learn and to do and to be.

FUN PROJECTS

God Wipes Away the Sin

On the chalkboard, draw a picture of a heart with a picture of an eye inside it. Explain to the child that when his heart is clean, it is like a clean window pane, and his spiritual eyes can see through to understand what is going on around him. When the heart is dirty

(illustrated by patting a dusty eraser over the picture), his spiritual eyes cannot see out the heart's window. Explain how when we confess our sin, God cleanses our heart (illustrated by wiping away the chalk dust with an eraser or damp cloth), and we can see God. Talk about how seeing God in Matthew 5:8 means to be able to see as God sees and to understand what is going on in our lives from God's point of view.

Ministering to the Unborn

"And it came about that when Elizabeth heard Mary's greeting, the baby leaped in her womb; and Elizabeth was filled with the Holy Spirit."

Luke 1:41-44, along with other Scriptures, makes it clear that babies have a capacity for spiritual discernment before birth. For that reason, it is important to minister to their spiritual needs. Marilyn noticed with our first baby that he had a strong response to music while still in the womb—uncomfortably strong, in fact. When he heard Doug Oldham sing, poor Mommy nearly bounced out of her seat.

So, we know that playing and singing good Christian music communicates with the child.

Reading Scripture aloud is another important method also. Both Mom and Dad should read to the baby. The parents' emotional and spiritual conflicts will have an effect on the child too, so this is one more reason that all problems between spouses should be cleared up immediately.

If I may risk digression, the welfare of the unborn baby is a good reason among many others that parents should teach and help their adolescents to learn, gain, and maintain financial freedom. The biggest pressure on most young couples is financial pressure. If parents would train their children properly and help them to get established, as they should, nearly all young married couples could enjoy the rare luxury of bringing their babies into a home without money problems. Would not you have loved it? Check out Proverbs 19:14 in reference to this.

36

Rock'n'Talk

Even a newborn loves to be rocked and talked to. Especially on your first one, when you have lots of time and not so many responsibilities, get in the habit of putting your family first. Rock in your rocker and chat with your child. Tell him you love him. Tell him Jesus made him, how special he is, and what wonderful plans God has for his life. Tell him how thankful you are to be his Mommy and how the Lord has been preparing you all your life to do this wonderful job. Talk to him about how Jesus designed him uniquely with high and heavenly purposes in mind, and how He suffered on a cross for his sins 2,000 years before she ever made her first mistake. You may be surprised one day to learn how much your little one internalized of all the lovely fellowship in the Lord, that you used to share in that old rocking chair.

Metaditation

37

Teach your children the principles of meditation.

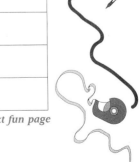

One good way is to have them quote a Bible verse that is meaningful to them and then ask them how it applies to their life. Another good tool is paraphrasing. Have the child write out a verse or passage, then rewrite it in his own words, changing each major word in the passage to a synonym.

Here are some sections of Scripture dealing with various topics. Help the child choose a passage suitable to his personal needs.

Topic	Scripture
Dealing with temptation	James 1
Insight into everyday problems	Proverbs
Self-acceptance	Psalm 139
Conquering fears	Psalm 91:17
Meditation	Psalm I, Joshua I

Continued on the very next fun page

Continued from the previous fun page

Overcoming worry	Philippians 4
Foundational teachings of Christ	Matthew 5,6,7
Values	Colossians 3
Conflicts of old and new natures	Romans 5,6,7
Controlling the tongue	James 4
Understanding chastening	Hebrews 12
Understanding God's Will	Romans 12
Real love	I Corinthians 13
Insights into faith	Hebrews 11
Dealing with suffering	I Peter 3
Dealing with emotions	Psalms*

*It has been said that the Book of Psalms contains the whole spectrum of human emotions, with the earlier part of each chapter laying groundwork or stating a problem, and

39

the concluding verse or verses giving a Godly perspective on the manner.

Scripture Saturation

Consider having a Bible theme for the decor in each room. We are not talking about a lot of money; that will make little difference in your effectiveness in saturating the home. You can use homemade materials and projects. It is more beneficial to make home furnishings that reflect the LORD than to buy them, especially if parents and children are involved together.

Suggested Themes

Room	Scripture Theme
Living Room	God's promises
Kitchen	God's provision
Bedroom	Husband's and wife's respon-sibilities, genuine love
Girl's Room	Character of a godly woman
Boy's Room	Character of a man of God

40

Character Sketch Quilts

A patchwork quilt teaching great Biblical character qualities

Marilyn outdid herself with this idea. Inspired by the *Character Sketches* books from Institute in Basic Life Principles, she created for each child a patchwork quilt teaching Biblical character qualities. She made the quilts of three colors of squares—one white or off-white that has a picture of one of the *Character Sketches* animals on it done in Vogart tube paints, a type of liquid embroidery. She used a heat-transfer pencil to trace the outline of the animal from the book then ironed it onto a quilt square and colored it in with paints. Above the animal in the same square is written the quality the animal demonstrates; underneath is written the definition of the quality given in *Character Sketches*. On the reverse side of the quilt, exactly in back of the animal picture square, is a Bible verse reflecting the quality. On the front you could also include the name of the person mentioned in *Character Sketches* as demonstrating or violating that character quality. You can use an old blanket, or the

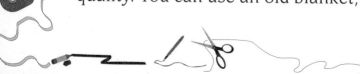

batting inside the quilt, and a sheet for backing. We tied the quilts with yarn. Marilyn's quilts have squares of animal pictures and 18 squares of two different colors, e.g. red and blue or light blue and dark blue.

Biography Curtains

We have done curtains several different ways. One way is to make curtains from sheets. Trace coloring book pictures with a heat transfer pencil onto the curtains and color them in with tube paints. Go back to the Christian book shop where you found all these other things we've told you to get, and pick up a good Bible story coloring book to supply you with Bible characters for the curtain stories. Another mode of transferring the pictures is by using fabric crayons and ironing on the picture from that. The advantage of this over other methods is that the colors are a little brighter. Read the curtains with or to the children daily or periodically to teach them about the Bible hero's life and to inculcate the lesson to be learned from that person.

Character Quality Curtains

This year we are trying to teach the 48 basic character qualities in *Character Sketches* to our children. We found a Bible character example of each of the qualities digging through several different coloring books, and let the children color them in. We ironed the pictures onto the curtains and wrote the quality above the picture, and the definition and verse reference below the picture. Every few days Marilyn and the younger kids all go into the bedroom and sit on the floor. She lets each child choose a picture. Then they talk about the Bible example person and character quality and go over the definition.

Wall Plaques

Elsewhere in this book we describe the *Jesus and the Children* plaques. Here are some more ideas for meaningful plaques on various spiritual themes. Marylin has found two good products for finishing decoupage plaques, and they are available at most craft stores. at least in our area. They are Art Podge and Mod

Podge. They are very easy materials to work with, requiring only one coat before applying the picture and two after. Use them or your favorite medium on some of the following plaque ideas:

Plaque Theme	Resources
Basic principle plaque	Use the basic principles taught in the IBYC basic seminar.
Jesus plaque	Find a good sketch or print of the LORD.
Meaning of name plaques	Find or make a rendering of the child's name and its spiritual meaning.
Miscellaneous ideas	Church bulletins, Ideals magazine, and old Sunday School material all may supply good pictures and themes. Religious greeting cards are often good, too.

Pillow Shams

We have pillow shams for the boys with the meaning of their names on them. For Mom there is one bearing the words of I Peter 3:1a, 4 and mine has I Peter 3:7. We once had a quilt with the words of I Corinthians 13.

44

Bureau Scarf

We put Psalms 25:12–14 and 22:30 on a scarf for the top of our dresser.

Tablecloths
Spiritual nutrition!

Make them from sheets and tube paints. There are a number of Bible ideas you can use; we had one reflecting a manger scene at Christmas. You could use the four food groups: Bread of Life, milk of the Word, spiritual meat, fruit of the Spirit, etc. Different seasons of the year suggest themes.

Throw Pillows

Our kids made throw pillows with Bible verses on them. Materials are sheets and fabric crayons.

45

Little Girl Quilt
Using the qualities of a godly woman theme

Marilyn made our daughter Katie a quilt using one of the Precious Moments coloring books Marilyn found at the Christian book shop. Using a heat transfer pencil, they traced the coloring book pictures onto hearts cut out of a pink sheet, then ironed them on. Then they colored them with tube paints. At the top of the heart above the picture, they wrote a Bible character quality. Below the heart, they wrote the definition of that quality. Because the quilt was for a little girl, they chose to use qualities of a godly woman for the theme. Marilyn made up a story about each picture, using our then three youngest family members—Katie, age 4; Matthew, age 2; and Emily, age 1—as characters in the story. The hearts are zig-zag seam onto a rosebud sheet. Every now and then, and sometimes every day, Mom would go over the quilt with Katie, retelling the story related to each picture.

46

Lamp Shades
Shine the Light!

If you will paint or pin a Scripture verse onto a lamp shade in your child's room, he or she will have a reminder of the LORD that can grab his attention when it comes on. One idea might be Matthew 5:14, "Ye are the light of the world." (KJV) Any room in the house might benefit by this.

Magazine Rack

Psalm 101:3 can be stained, painted, or wood burned onto the front of your living room magazine rack as a reminder to be careful what you look at. "I will set no wicked thing before mine eyes." (KJV)

Milk Can

If you can find an old 10-gallon milk can like the ones the farmers sent their milk to the dairy in when I was a kid, you can do a neat project Marilyn did for our living room. She

47

painted the can shiny black and applied a big decal of a golden eagle to the front. She then wrote Isaiah 40:31 underneath: " But they that wait upon the LORD shall renew their strength, they shall mount up with wings as eagles..." (KJV)

Miscellaneous Ideas

Besides wall plaques, you can build Scripture into your home decor using some of these ideas: Verses on the mirror (James 1:23-25), cross-stitch polydomes, embroidery, or to give the kids a thrill, let them color Bible verses onto construction paper and illustrate them with crayons, and then frame the masterpieces and hang them in conspicuous places throughout the house.

Bible Flash Cards
This was one of Marilyn's earliest and best ideas

Using 5x7 cards or pieces cut from construction paper, let the child color a stick-figure picture on the paper to illustrate a Bible

48

verse. One of Rickey's favorites when he was about two years old was one from Proverbs in the Living Bible paraphrase: "The lazy man is full of excuses; 'I can't get up and go to work,' he says, 'I might meet a lion in the street and be killed!'" On the front of the card, have just the picture. In this example, we had a picture of a man on a bed, dreaming of a lion (lion in a thought balloon above the man's head. Show the cards' front sides only to the child. As he sees the picture he remembers the verse associated and quotes it to you. When he quotes it, hand the card to him. He feels as if he just won a prize, and when he has the whole stack in his hands he will swell up like a wet sponge. By the way, it would be a good idea to have the Scripture reference on the front of the card above the picture and the verse written on the back.

ABC Men Chart

We let the boys color pictures of men from a Bible coloring book then assigned them names following the letters of the alphabet (e.g., A-Abraham, B-Balaam, C-Caleb). We

wrote under each picture a character quality the man either manifested or violated. We hung these pictures around the walls of their bedroom, near the ceiling, and went through them daily with the boys.

Bible Tapes
This is without question one of the most spiritually profitable projects we have ever done with our children.

We have achieved excellent results for several years. It has been said that the last thoughts on our minds at night will be on our minds all night and the first thoughts we think the next day. For this reason, bedtime and nap time are perhaps the very best times of all to play tapes of Scripture. Our Joshua, when he was five years old, loved the Gospels in the New International Version. He usually listened to them at both nap time and bedtime. The result was that after a few weeks, he amazed us with his memorization. Mom or Dad would start a verse from one of the Gospels, and little Josh would finish it and usually go on. These tapes will fill your child's mind with God's thoughts and give him proper food for meditation while he is resting or sleeping.

One good type of approach is to get the dramatized New Testament tapes, which utilize different voices to read the words of people involved in conversations, etc. My brother who once worked at a Christian radio station, has recorded for our kids many fine Scripture tapes, some of which have verses interspersed with music, another excellent idea. A good method, and perhaps the best, is to have Mom and Dad read Scripture into the tape recorder for the children's tapes. In this way, the kids can be read to by Daddy even when he is at work. Bible story tapes are great. The commercially produced set of Bible tapes narrated by Arthur Scourby are very good. Tapes of Scriptures dealing with a theme or topic are good: read into the recorder verses about obedience, godliness, purity, truthfulness, kindness, words, thankfulness, etc. Music tapes are something we all love at our house. And there are plenty of good ones made for children in particular. Scripture songs are preferred for our kids. Develop the ministry of your older kids by encouraging

51

them to make tapes for their younger siblings.
Our boys love to do this and the babies think
it is wonderful. Do your children have fears at
bedtime when the lights go out? Daddy's voice
reading Psalm 91 will help. Scripture tapes at
bedtime, by the way, are an excellent method
of combating nightmares.

Scripture Songs and Spiritual Music

*Another excellent way for your children to
memorize and meditate on God's Word is to
learn Scripture songs.*

You will hear your children singing
Scripture instead of contemporary television
and radio garbage as they go about their play.
Our Matthew, alias Boomie, at age two would
sing At the Cross and other old hymns as well
as several contemporary Scriptural children's
songs. Of course it will be necessary to
carefully screen the music you buy for your
children. Marilyn and I are extremely
conservative in our choice of music, both for
us and our children. We have liked the
following records and tapes, so we recommend
them to you, with the stipulation that all tapes

and records must be reviewed by the parent
before turning them over to the child.

Recommended Selections

Title	Artist/Publisher
Sounds of Praise	Gospel Light Publications, Ventura, CA 93806 ©1979
God's Kids	Rick Powell, Zondervan Corp. 1415 Lake Dr. SE, Grand Rapids, MI 49506 ©1978
Songs for Babies and Toddlers	Gospel Light Publications, Ventura, CA 93806 ©1979
Children Sing to the Lord	Gospel Light Publications, Ventura, CA 93806 ©1979
Sing 'n' Tell (This record is excellent— tells a Scripture story and then sings a song about it.)	Master's Press, 20 Mills St. Kalamazoo, Mi. 49001 ©1971
I'm a Promise	Bill Gaither Trio, The Benson Co. 625 Broadway, Nashville, TN. 37203
Music Machine	Candle Co. Music, Sparrow Records, Canoga Park, CA ©1977
Bullfrogs and Butterflies*	Candle Co. Music, Sparrow Records, Canoga Park, CA ©1977
Critter County*	Christine Wyrtzen Loveland Records 6278 Branch Hill Loveland, OH 45140 ©1984

Recommended: (But with some content we did not like)

53

We also like the *Maranatha Singers' Praise Albums* numbers 1-6. This is mostly softer music, and for the whole family. Each of these albums, I believe, is available both in vocal and instrumental form. Most of these albums contained one or more songs we were not crazy about and later albums in the series were generally too "contemporary" for our taste.

We have found that home-educated kids tend to like whatever music their parents do, and ours enjoy music by Doug Oldham, choral groups, and many others. Jana Getz' book of Scripture songs for kids *Merry Voices Happy Songs*, is about the best I have ever seen in children's' songs for singing on their own or with an autoharp. You can write your own Scripture songs if you will take the time. Speaking of autoharps, be sure and get one for your children if you possibly can. Our kids have taught themselves to play, and one of the boys at age eleven could play about any song you could sing to him, whether he had ever heard it before or not. The instrument makes a very nice and full sound. They are reasonably priced, and tuning and service are generally inexpensive.

54

The Daily Proverb
The Bible contains 31 Proverbs—a Proverb for each day of the month.

Each day, have the children read through the chapter of Proverbs corresponding to the day of the month: For example, Proverbs 14 on June 14th. They then choose one verse in the chapter that stands out to them. Then have them paraphrase the verse and write a prayer about it to the LORD, asking Him to help them instill it into their lives. These sheets are kept in their life notebooks.

Memoreward
If your children have never committed whole chapters of Scripture to memory, you have a treat in store that may bring tears to your eyes.

Our most recent memorization goal for our kids is Matthew 5, 6 and 7. Some of the kids have already completed the assignment; the younger ones are still at it. Set goals that are reasonable according to the ability of the child. When the goal is reached, give the child a worthy reward. Suggestions could include a new Bible, a Bible story book, a copy of The

Picture Bible (kids love it), a Christian record or tape, a Bible puzzle, or their own personal tropical fish or house plant. For special accomplishments, such as when all of the children have reached demanding goals in memorization, have an awards ceremony with refreshments and surprise gifts.

Scripture Wheel

The kids isolated some areas of conflict that were special problems to them and Marilyn helped them look up a Scripture dealing with each one. The verses were written on a circle of poster board about 18 inches across, divided into "pie slices" with a topical verse in each slice. This was then covered by a slightly smaller circle of poster board and the two pinned together in the middle on the wall so that the back circle stayed stationary and the front one could be rotated. On the exposed edge of the back circle Marilyn wrote a problem. Then in the same slice but closer to the center of the circle so that it was covered by the front circle, she wrote the verse that provided God's answer to the problem. She left a slice cut out of the

front circle so that one of the answer verses was exposed. Then the kids all sit together watching while Mom points out one of the problems on the outer edge of the back circle. The kids try to remember the verse that deals with that area. When they have tried to quote the verse, she then lets them check for themselves by turning the front wheel so that the missing slice turns to the verse they are looking for, which is in the same slice as the problem on the back wheel. The answer verse is then exposed, thus letting the kids know whether they were right.

Open Bible Memory Flash Cards

Cut the shape of an open Bible from construction paper. On the front write a topic area and the reference to a Scripture verse dealing with that topic area. On the back, write out the verse. Example: front, "When tempted to be afraid...Psalm 91:10,11"; on the back, "No evil will befall you, nor will any plague come near your tent. For He will give His angels charge concerning you, to guard you in all your ways." (KJV)

Then cover the "Bibles" with contact paper and use them to learn the verses. Check different versions of Scripture and use the one that best expresses the particular verse for your child's understanding.

Some Examples

Topic	Scripture Reference
Success is promised to us if...	Joshua 1:8
Does doing this offend others?	I Corinthians 10:31–33
Dealing with others who mistreat us	Luke 6:27,28
Success is promised to us if...	Joshua 1:8
I have a chance to do a good thing, should I take it?	James 4:17
When you are tempted...	I Corinthians 10:13
Foolish or harmful words...	Ephesians 4:29
When tempted to worry...	Philippians 4:6,7
Wanting the best for myself...	Philippians 2:3,4
When tempted to gripe about others	James 5:9-11

Continued on the very next fun page

58

Continued from the previous fun page

Topic	Scripture Reference
Griping and arguing...	Phiippians 12:1
How can I keep from sinning?	Psalm 119:9,11
Wrong thoughts...	Philippians 4:8
When tempted with pride...	James 4:6

Boast Board
Named for Rickey's favorite animal characteristic—the Lion!

When Rickey was little, Marilyn made him a little plywood board with pictures of animals glued on the front and finished with decoupage. Under the picture of each animal they wrote a Bible verse referring to a characteristic displayed by that animal. (The Lion was Rickey's favorite; hence the name "Boast Board".)

Some Examples

Animal	Trait	Reference	Verse
Elephant	Long memory	Psalm 119:11	"Thy Word have I hid in mine heart" (KJV)
Lion	Proud	2 Corinthians 10:17	"He who boasts, let him boast in the Lord"(NASB)
Fox	Sly	Philipians 1.3:2	"Beware of dogs, beware of evildo-ers" (KJV)
Kangaroo (Cartoon kangaroo wearing boxing gloves)	Fighting	Ephesians 4:26	"Be angry and sin not, let not the sun go down on your anger" (NASB)
Bear (Cartoon baby bear has hand over heart)	Inner concern	Revelation 3:20	"Behold, I stand at the door and knock" (NASB)
Monkey	Imitator	Ephesians 5:1	"Therefore be imitators of God as beloved chil-dren" (NASB)

Sowing and Reaping Board

We made a spring bulletin board to help us understand that whatever we sow, that will we reap. The kids each made a pretty spring flower of construction paper and attached it to the board, then drew its root, bulb or seed, and stem. On the bulb or seed they quote what quality was sown and on the flower they quote what quality Scripture says will be reaped as a result of sowing that seed. On the flower's stem they wrote the Scripture reference.

For Example:

Flower Part	Bulb	Stem	Flower
What was sown & reaped	Love	1John 4:19	More Love
	Kind Words	Proverbs 16:24	Enjoyment & Health
	Joyful Heart	Proverbs 15:13	Cheerful Face

Topical Proverbs

This can be a part of your "classwork." Rearrange the entire book of Proverbs according to topics. Start at the beginning and make vertical columns on sheets of paper, one for each topic. To keep the project simple, make the topic areas general.

Book Screening

Scripture says we are to set no wicked thing before our eyes in Psalm 101:3. Yet it is startling how many Christian parents let their children watch television and read anything they get their hands on, unless it is obviously pornographic. Even home-educating parents are often very lax in checking up on and screening what their children read. It is not just that which is immoral that we must eliminate from our kids attention; but there are countless books on store and library shelves that are simply profanity and foolishness. Our family does not read ghost stones, wild fantasy, or books that build false values. That would include many young people's books about sports, cars, or dating. We screen all the books before they come home from the library and if we buy the kids a book or one is given to them, we check it and remove or expunge any objectionable parts. We have even had to throw away some gift books outright. By the standards of most people, we are very conservative in our choice of reading material for our children. But I feel that it would be hard to overemphasize the critical importance of keeping a child's mind protected from impurity. If you are one who would join the public schools in warning me about going too far in "protecting" my children, let me point out

62

the fruits of their system as my answer. You would not let your children eat garbage, and you try to limit their intake of foods that are just not profitable so that they do not spoil their appetites for that which they need most. Be at least that selective with their spiritual and intellectual diet.

Doctrine for Kids
Here are some good children's books dealing with doctrinal things

Children's Bible Basics Series
A series by Carolyn Nystrom, published by Moody Press. To get these books check the Christian bookstore or write Moody Press, Chicago.

Titles
- *Who Is Jesus*
- *Who Is God*
- *The Holy Spirit in Me*
- *Growing Jesus' Way*
- *What Is Prayer?*
- *What Is a Church?*
- *What Is a Christian?*
- *Why Do I Do Things Wrong?*
- *What Happens When I Die?*

63

Leading Little Ones to God
by Marian M. Schoolland, Eerdmans Publishing
Co. Grand Rapids, Michigan 1962.
Containing short devotional stories, easily
understandable on basic Bible doctrine.

Daily Kids' Devotions

Do daily Bible reading and record God's
promises, reproofs, blessings, wisdom, and
special encouragement.

Daily Devotional Diaries

We used notebooks. The kids pasted
pictures on the front. We divided the book into
sections. Examples of divisions might include
prayer requests and answers, daily Proverbs
chapter, daily Scripture reading record,
insights, etc.

Character Studies

You may want to study a character quality each month, or just on an occasional basis.

Character training has little effect without application, so develop projects to apply what your children are learning and to help them learn it.

Here are some books you will find helpful in teaching Godly character to your children:

Character Sketches vol. I,II,III
Institute in Basic Life Principles, Box 1, Oak Brook, IL

Children's Book of Character Building
by Ron and Rebekah Coriel. Fleming H. Revell Co. Old Tappan, NJ, 1980. Gives a good definition of eight character qualities, a story of the quality illustrated in the Bible, at home. at school, and at play. Lists several projects for application.

Character Builders
by Ron and Rebekah Coriell. Fleming H. Revell Co. Old Tappan, NJ, 1981. These are a series

of books of 32 pages or so each, all dealing with Godly character. They give Bible stories, Hero of the Faith stories, and stories at home and school. Each book covers three character qualities. They sell at present for less than $1 each. They come in 3 divisions.

Titles

- *Eyeglass Series: Young children*
- *Spyglass Series: Ages 8-11*
- *Looking Glass Series: Ages 12-15*

What Does the Bible Say?

by Jane Belk Moncure, The Child's World, Elgin, IL 60220, 1980. There is a series of character search quizzes produced by the Association of Christian Schools International. Write to them at P.O. Box 4097, Whittier, Calif. 90607. These are geared to school grade levels but of course use whatever level material your child seems to do best with. Institute in Basic Life Principles has an excellent game to teach character qualities, called Character Clues. See Character Sketches section for publishing information.

66

A Place for Everything
The idea is to have a place for everything so everything can be put in its place.

When we studied the quality of orderliness, we used the time to get the house in order. Part of this may be adding shelves to the kids' closet, buying plastic boxes or dishpans to hold toys, etc. You can label the boxes for certain kinds of toys or other things. For little children who cannot read yet, use a picture of a toy truck on the box for cars, etc. Make it easy rather than hard for them to be orderly and obedient.

Star Charts

Make a chart showing each of the kids' responsibilities: feed fish, pick up room, make bed, help with dishes, etc. When the child has done his jobs for the day, give him a star to stick on his chart.

Proverbs Character Studies

This is a good idea for Mom and Dad to do on their own and then share with the kids. Or, with the older children, you can go through the studies together. This is a good opportunity to teach children to use a concordance and make a chart of their findings. For younger children, give them the Scripture reference and let them just look up the verses. There are at least 64 types of negative/positive character-type contrasts in the book of Proverbs. It is suggested that they be studied in contrasting pairs if appropriate, and charted in some form.

Sample Method

Character Type	Scripture Reference	Charac- teristics	Instructions to or about him
Sluggard	Proverbs 22:13	Makes excuses	Fill In

Some character types in Proverbs
- ◆ diligent/slothful
- ◆ wicked/righteous
- ◆ prudent/naive

- ◆ talebearer/faithful witness
- ◆ liar/truthful
- ◆ backslider
- ◆ arrogant
- ◆ deceiver
- ◆ just/unjust
- ◆ proud,/humble
- ◆ foolish/wise
- ◆ strange woman/virtuous woman

The purpose of the study is to teach ourselves and our children to discern character strengths and weaknesses in ourselves and those around us, and know what Scriptural directives are for dealing with different types of people.

Is this really necessary? Consider how many times you have heard someone say after being influenced to foolish actions by a con artist, led astray by wicked friends, or marrying or hiring a person with serious character flaws—"Oh, if only I had known what he was really like!"

Section 3
Building A Hunger
For Righteousness

*Blessed are
they which
do hunger and thirst
after righteousness:
for they shall
be filled.*

—*MATTHEW 5:6 KJV*

72

*I*F YOU GREW up with a taste for junk food and are now trying to wean yourself onto a healthier diet, you have come to realize that you'd have been better off to develop a taste for wholesome foods in the beginning.

The same applies to our mental and spiritual health. Most of us grew up on a diet of television, secular music, unworthy activities, and wrong companionship.

We cannot turn back the clock and start our own lives all over again, but those of us with children can see that they do not grow up as we did, with an insatiable appetite for the junk food of this world. It has been observed that those things to which we are often exposed are the things for which we build a tolerance and a taste. For that reason, it is our job as parents to create for our kids a life menu that majors on spiritual health food. Just as my kids now like their mother's bran muffins while I would rather have toast and jelly, so we can feed them that which will build in them a liking for that which is spiritually good for them rather than garbage.

Building A Hunger For Righteousness

The projects you will find in this section are designed to provide you with ideas for your children to do to make spiritual things tasteful. It should be a joyful activity to serve the LORD, who died a Man of sorrows in order that our joy might be full. We hope these ideas will prime your creativity pump as you go far beyond them in designing projects to give your children a hunger and thirst for God's righteousness.

FUN PROJECTS

Daily Devotions

Have older kids read through the Old Testament. They can do so at the rate of 3 chapters a day for 1 year. Have them look for principles of truth obeyed or violated in the lives of Bible characters and make notes of the results. For example, Abraham obeyed God in offering Isaac and received his son back with added blessing. On the other side of the coin, Abraham also compromised his morality at Sarah's suggestion and reaped her rebellion

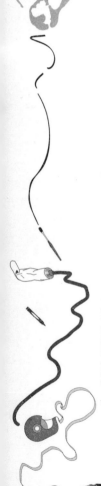

74

and contempt as well as lasting conflict in his lineage.

Biographies

Read with the kids, or encourage them to read, life stories of great Christians. Scripture promises that the testimony (eyewitness account) of the LORD is sure, making wise the simple. That is why it is important for children to read both in and out of Scripture the workings of God in the lives of different people, particularly those who are good examples. I have seen a series of children's books documenting the lives of famous Americans from a Christian viewpoint, and they looked excellent. Many people are not aware that George Washington and Robert E. Lee, for instance, were strong followers of Christ. You may find good material in the stories of preachers, missionaries, martyrs, etc. I have been particularly impressed and blessed by biographies of George Muller, George Whitefield, Charles Finney, John and Charles Wesley, and others. We have had the children

75

do "book reports" using a homemade form
called "Treasure Hunt for Godly Character."

Sunday Box
*Your Sunday Box should make your family
look forward to Sunday*

Isaiah 58:13,14 makes this promise: "If
thou turn away thy foot from the Sabbath,
from doing thy pleasure on my holy day; and
call the Sabbath a delight, the holy of the Lord,
honourable; and shalt honour him, not doing
thine own pleasure, nor speaking thine own
words: Then shalt thou delight thyself in the
Lord and I will cause thee to ride on the high
places of the earth, and feed thee with the
heritage of Jacob thy father: for the mouth
of the Lord hath spoken it."

You have no doubt heard stories of the
traditional abuses of the injunction to honor
the Sabbath: Do not move around too much,
do not get too loud, and above all do not have
any fun. That, of course, is mostly ancient
history, something our parents tell about.
Nowadays the pendulum has swung toward

the opposite extreme. Sundays are generally spent, other than going to church, in whatever pursuits happen to appeal to us. By ridding ourselves of a burdensome old tradition, it seems we have lost sight of an important principle that the practices originally represented: People need one day a week to concentrate on the things of the LORD. It is not a matter of what we should not he doing, but of what we should be doing. We will be spiritually healthier if we will spend a day a week thinking about the LORD, letting other things step aside for that which is most important and therefore requires our undivided attention sometimes. But even if I am content to spend the day in spiritual pursuits, how do I get my children to do the same?

Put together a Sunday Box. Explain thoroughly to your children the reason for observing a special LORD's Day. Then find a large box and fill it with delightful things for the kids to enjoy doing on Sunday. Be sure to let the kids take part in choosing things to put in the box. It should contain a variety of interesting things and the contents will need

Building A Hunger For Righteousness

to be changed from time to time in order to keep it fascinating. If you use creativity in stuffing the Sunday Box, enclose a wide variety of contents, psych the kids up about it and allow the Box to be open only on Sunday you will be surprised to find how much your family comes to look forward to Sunday. What to include? Only those things which are very interesting to your children but cause their minds to turn to the LORD. You could use special Bible story books for Dad to read with the family. Records or tapes of Christian music for children or Bible stories. Dollies dressed in Bible costumes. Bible games, Bible puzzles, Bible quiz materials, Christian biographies, Christian books on topics of interest to Mom and Dad. For a treat, on Saturday bake a Bible cake and put in the box for next day. Christian toys such as wooden Noah's ark and animals, Bible coloring books, flannel graph Bible characters. The list is as long as you care to make it. The thing to keep in mind is that all Sunday Box contents must meet two criteria: It must be spiritually oriented and it must be fascinating to the kids. Your Sunday Box should make your family look forward to

78

Sunday instead of dreading it, as many of us
often do.

Family Night Bible Quiz
*Have a family member read a chapter of
Scripture and then ask questions about it.*

You may already have a family night each
week. We enjoy family nights, perhaps most
of all in winter. We have a fireplace in our
living room and the room's small size adds to
the cozy feeling. One of our favorite forms for
family night is to heat a pan of milk by the fire
for hot chocolate and pop popcorn. Then as
we indulge we sit around and enjoy a Bible
quiz. Usually I go around the room asking
questions off the top of my head, starting with
the youngest family member present. Of
course, the questions are geared to the age
bracket. If the youngest cannot answer the
question, I move to the next youngest and ask
him. If he gets the answer right then I go back
to the youngest and give him a question I think
he can answer. Obviously, when the youngest
is very young—say, a toddler—the questions
have to be very simple: "Who is the Son of

God?" etc. The older kids are very hard to fool and I always dread someone's suggesting that the kids take a turn asking and Dad a turn answering. You can vary the routine by using questions taken from Bible games. There is now a trivia game based on Scripture. Or you can have a family member read a chapter of Scripture and then ask questions about it.

Cloth Bible Book

Marilyn made a really neat little quiet time book for our two-year-old out of fabric scraps using patterns from a book called *Busy Books: Patterns for Cloth Books* by Janet Sage. It is published by Concordia Publishing House, St. Louis, Mo., 1946. This book contains patterns enough for 4 or 5 busy books and all are based on a Bible theme. The author has 4 different books, all containing several cloth book ideas. The one Marilyn made teaches the child colors as well as how to zip and unzip, button and unbutton, tie and untie, etc. There are Noah's Ark patterns Coat of Many Colors, Isaac on the Altar (featuring: a Velcro-backed Isaac to be replaced by a Velcro-backed ram) and a number of other ideas.

Example Stories

This is good for family devotions, among many other things.

Read a chapter of Scripture, perhaps Proverbs, and pick out a phrase or whole verse. Or, let the kids pick out a verse from that chapter or elsewhere in Scripture. Then take the verse or phrase and tell a story about it. It is easier to tell interesting stories than you may think. Use a true story from your childhood or a story about someone you know or read about. Use a story from the Bible. A story from the newspaper. Do not use a story from television. If you have the silly thing in your home at all, at least do not build your children's interest in it.

For instance, Proverbs 27:23,24: "Be thou diligent to know the state of thy flocks, and look well to thy herds: for riches are not for ever: and doth the crown endure to every generation?" (KJV)

Building A Hunger For Righteousness

81

I remember when I was a boy on the farm, we had a herd of cows in a pasture over the hill from the house. I was responsible to walk over the hill every day and check on the cows to make sure none of them was sick, and that they were all there and so forth. I remember the grass was high, up to my waist.

It was always chilly in the morning, and the dew on the grass made my pants wet almost to my belt. Funny how I recall, but you know I always got irritated that the weed seeds stuck between my toes and itched. Well, one morning I ran back there to check on the cows before school. When I got to where I expected to find them, the herd was nowhere around. There was a big, dead tree lying across the fence where it had fallen during the night. It had knocked down the wire and two fence posts. Now cows seem to always want something different than they have. People are that way sometimes too, aren't they? (Pause for a response but beware letting it get out of hand.) "Well, our cows had decided that the grass looked a little greener on the other side of the fence, so they had all walked through the gap the tree had made in the fence

82

when it fell on it, and into our neighbor's pasture. I ran and got my dad and brother, and we spent three hours trying to round up forty-some cows and head them back through that gap in the fence." (Here you could embellish a bit by telling them about some of the adventures you had running around in that pasture.) "But we had to do it. If we hadn't, our cows could have gotten mixed up with some of our neighbor's, and we might not have been able to tell some of our animals from his. We might have lost some of our cows because we were not sure which was which. But we got 'em all back because we always checked them every day. We looked well to our herds. And another good result was that I missed half a day of school."

King Solomon Birthday Party
Why not add a Bible emphasis to your birthday party?

We usually prefer to have family only at birthdays, but many people like to have friends over. We did this idea once and invited some of the kids' friends to join us for the

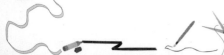

83

celebration. The idea is to give a Scripture emphasis to each portion of the program. We played "Solomon Says" (Simon Says), let each child make himself a king's crown of construction paper decorated with glitter and a stick-on picture of Jesus, and wrote "Happy is the man that findeth wisdom" across the top. We sang Scripture songs, especially on the topic of wisdom. We also had a Bible quiz with questions concerning wisdom. On birthdays, the birthday boy or girl serves the refreshments to the other children because we want to remind them that the greatest among us will be the servant of all.

Walking by the Way

Deuteronomy 6:6,7 tells us that we are to have the words of God on our hearts and to teach them to our children, talking of them, among other times when we walk by the way. We seldom walk anywhere as a family, but riding from place to place in the car provides an opportunity for good conversation. Some ideas: Take turns telling about one good thing

84

that happened today. Sing godly songs. List
some blessings.

Gratefulness Letters
*Letters are due to any person who has helped
your child: grandparent, friend, pastor, Sunday
school teacher, or whoever.*

Everybody wants to be appreciated. One
excellent way we can express appreciation—
and in so doing teach others to express it,
too—is to write special letters to those by
whose influence we have benefited. We adults
should do this much more often than we do,
and our kids certainly need to learn to do it
early. Perhaps if more attention were given to
this and like sentiments, the "Me Generation"
would never have been. Letters are due to any
person who has helped your child:
grandparent, friend, pastor, Sunday school
teacher, or whoever. Our kids wrote a
thankfulness letter to our neighbor, Mrs. Lusk,
who will surely make the Guinness Book for
good neighbors. She is one of the kindest,
friendliest, most cheerful ladies we have ever
known, and a marvelous contrast to some

Building A Hunger For Righteousness

of the neighbors we have all had. One thing of which you can be sure: Whomever you write to, this is one piece of mail that will make his day.

Plays

Let your kids make up and perform plays. Our kids like to do nature plays. We have had some very convincing renditions of bears and wolves right in our own basement. Bible stories are very good, of course.

Where in the Bible Game

Let the kids make little shapes of open Bibles out of construction paper. On the front of one Bible, write Genesis 1. On the back, write the main topic of the chapter: Creation. Other examples: Psalm 23, the LORD is my Shepherd. Deuteronomy 6, Parents Teach Your Children. John 15, the Vine and the Branches.

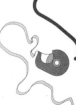

86

Flannel Graph Dolls

You can buy these dolls or let the kids make their own by cutting the figures from flannel. Cover a board with flannel to make your flannel graph, then let the children act out Bible stories with their dolls, the figures covered with homemade flannel Bible costumes.

Bible-Times Scrapbook

Your kids can make these neat little books from construction paper pages tied together with yarn and illustrated with Bible pictures. Of course some of these can be hand-drawn, but you can often get outdated Sunday school materials cheaply or free and use these as a source of pictures. Cut them out and paste onto pages. These books are good for taking to church as quiet entertainment for baby, and serve well as gifts to bedridden sick friends.

Building A Hunger For Righteousness

Bible Jigsaw Puzzles

Paste Bible pictures or maps (a good Bible geography lesson) onto cardboard or plywood. Then cut with a knife or saw into irregular shapes to make a puzzle, more and smaller pieces for the older child. Finish the wooden ones with varnish or decoupage lacquer.

Ironed Crayon Bible Verse Books

Let the children write Bible verses or illustrate stories in regular crayon on muslin cloth. Go over them with an iron, thus making them semi-permanent. Sew the sheets together for pages using a zigzag stitch.

Stained Glass Bible Verse Pictures

The children write a Bible verse and illustrate it in crayon on regular white paper. Then rub the picture with a cotton ball moistened with baby oil or mineral oil. Mount in a posterboard frame and hang in a window.

88

Sunlight will shine through, creating a stained glass effect.

Noah's Ark Room Theme

We made a Noah's ark room for one of our children during the infant years. We papered one wall with Noah's ark wallpaper. You should be able to find some, especially if your town has a store that specializes in wallpaper. We decorated the room with macramé animals and gave them Bible names: Enoch the Elephant, Lazarus the Lion, etc. Marilyn made wall hangings of the ark and several animals; and even a rainbow.

You can get macramé animal patterns from a little book *Macramé Animal Art* published by Craft Publications Inc., 1450 Kelton Dr. Stone Mountain, Ga. 30083. For the stuffed art and animal wall hangings, Marilyn saw a picture of a set in a book, selling for around $75. She designed her own and made them for $7 or $8.

Building A Hunger For Righteousness

Wooden Noah's Ark

89

Design and build your own wooden Ark of plywood, then use a jigsaw or bandsaw to cut out animal shapes and Mr. and Mrs. Noah and their family from 1-inch lumber, such as regular 2x4 or 2x6 boards. Finish the ark and characters with paint. Vogart tube paints work well.

Wooden Bible Characters

Along the same line as the above idea, you can save some money on overpriced Christian toys by cutting other Bible figures from wood and decorating them yourselves. Kids usually love animals as well as people figures.

Bible Doll

Get a well-constructed doll for your daughter and sew different outfits for her to dress the dollie up as various Bible characters. If you have both male and female dolls, you can create your own Biblical doll society and

your child will move right in. Here an aside: We feel very strongly that some of the dolls promoted on TV, if not all of them, are designed to foster worldly values in your child. First, the ad itself is intended to create discontent with her present dolls and toys. Then, she is encouraged to get excited about cheap worldly notions of fashion so that she will cry for dozens of new outfits. In many cases, the advertising involves the relationship between some girl doll and her boyfriend doll, inspiring some of the sickening premature interest in sex and romance so prevalent nowadays even in very young children. We encourage you to make and/or equip your child's dolls.

Manger Scene Christmas Ornaments

Make bakers' clay by mixing 2 cups of salt with 1 cup of flour and enough water to make a dough like consistency. Roll out to desired thickness and cut into animal shapes, a manger, Joseph and Mary, etc. using a knife or cookie cutters if you can find them. Preheat oven to 250°, bake by placing figures on a cookie sheet and placing them in the

91

preheated oven but turning the heat off when placing them in. Let the figures stay in the oven all night, then paint with ceramic paints and spray with ceramic finish. Do not forget to punch a small hole for the hook before baking.

Names of Jesus Ornaments

This past Christmas the kids embroidered the names of Jesus (Messiah, LORD, The Word, etc.) on ornaments. The embroideries are put in circular plastic frames and hooks attached for hanging on the tree.

Clay-dough Bible Characters

Mix 1 cup of flour, 2 teaspoon of cream of tarter, I cup of water, food coloring, 1/2 cup of salt, 3 tablespoons of oil. Combine in pan. Stir constantly on medium heat until mixture forms a firm ball. Let cool. Store in airtight container. Use to make Bible characters. You can dry the forms and keep them if you wish. Of course the dough can be used for many other things as well.

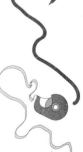

Section 4
Building
Self-Acceptance

*...Thou shalt
love thy neighbor
as thyself.*
—*MATTHEW 22:39 KJV*

94

*J*ESUS INSTRUCTED US *to love our neighbors as ourselves. This is not possible unless we have learned to love ourselves.*

The key to accepting and loving ourselves is to internalize the fact that God has created us according to a unique and special design, and that because we are significant to Him, we are truly significant.

Much of the conflict between children in schools stems from the fact that each child is a threat to the success of the others. To excel, you must do better than the other guy. You compete in academics, sports, social things, perhaps even in "spirituality." This fosters a spirit of competition, rather than God's desired attitude, cooperation.

This comparison also teaches a child to compare himself with others in other areas of achievement in order to evaluate himself. This is the reason that so many children have tremendous self-acceptance problems, which then continue into teen and adult years if not corrected. School, of course, is not the only

95

influence toward comparison as a standard. Parents are usually the first ones guilty of attacking their kids' character, thus damaging their ability to see themselves as important creations of a loving God.

The following projects will give you specific ways to help your child come to see that he is somebody special because he is special to God. Then he will be free from the pressure to beat others down in order to elevate himself. As he grows toward a Scriptural love for himself as God's creation, he grows toward being able to love others on the same basis.

FUN PROJECTS

Jesus Plaque

Artist Frances Hook has drawn a marvelous sketch of Jesus with a group of children. He is surrounded by them and is cupping one child's face in his hand and making eye contact with the child. Buy this

picture at your Christian bookstore, then make or buy a plaque board large enough to accommodate it. Carefully glue your own child's face into the picture from behind. To do this will require that you take a snapshot of your child from about 3 to 4 feet away, depending on your camera. It may help if while Daddy is taking the picture, Mommy stands in front of the child, smiling lovingly to help the child look up at about the right angle to look into the Lord's face in the plaque picture. Cover the hole with as many coats as needed of your favorite decoupage lacquer. We strongly suggest that you hang this picture above your child's bed so that his last thought at night and first in the morning can be of himself and Jesus looking intently at each other. The idea, of course, is to help the child internalize the fact of the Lord's individual love and concern for him.

Fabric Crayon T-Shirts

Purchase a package of fabric crayons at a bookstore, department store or craft shop. Select a garment that is at least 50% polyester

or the color will wash out. For a picture, we have chosen some excellent ones from the *Bethany Bible Coloring Books* from Bethany Fellowship, Minneapolis, Minn. 55438. For the purpose of teaching self-acceptance, we like the one that quotes Psalm 139:14 "I am fearfully and wonderfully made." It is to be found in *Psalms to Color* or *More Psalms to Color*; we forget which. But both books are from Bethany Fellowship and available at many Christian bookstores. The price printed on ours is $.59 or $.69, depending on the book. This project is most beneficial, albeit messier, if the child traces the picture and letters himself, rather than Mom doing it. In either case, outline the letters on the page with a darker crayon than they are colored in with. This is not necessary for the picture, but the letters will require it. Do your coloring on the back of the page in the coloring book. Otherwise, your picture and letters will come out backwards on the shirt. Once the coloring is complete, place the shirt on the ironing board encircling the board—that is, with the front of the garment on top of the ironing board and the back hanging below it. Otherwise, you will have the picture and words right on the front but also faintly on the back. Set your iron for COTTON and let it heat up thoroughly. Place a clean sheet of paper over the coloring book page and iron over that. As you iron, lift the corner of the page occasionally to check whether the color is transferring properly. If it is not, let your iron get slightly hotter and try some more. Lift only one corner at a time, or the page may move, resulting in smudged lines. With some practice, this is much easier than it may seem. This a wonderful rebuke to humanism—your child telling the world, "No, I should not have been aborted—God made me special !"

Spiritual Souvenirs
Save objects that bear special spiritual significance to your children.

Save simple articles of spiritual significance to you or your child. Deuteronomy 6, a great chapter for every parent, talks about the importance of spiritual symbolism to a child. In verses 6 through 9, Israel is told to think on God's words, talk of them, teach them to their children, and in 8 and 9 especially, we

are given some projects to serve as visible reminders of God. Verse 8, concerning wearing apparel, could apply to the above project very well. Another way to provide visible reminders of God and spiritual things is to save objects that bear special spiritual significance. Examples might include water in which the child was baptized, part of the cast he wore as a result of failing to use Godly wisdom, his first Bible, a letter from the man who was your pastor on the occasion of the child's birth, snapshots of the child involved in spiritual activities, etc. The list of possibilities is unending. The result of building an environment that makes your child aware of the things of God is mentioned in Deuteronomy 6:20 "And when thy son asketh thee in time to come, saying, What mean the testimonies, and the statutes, and the judgments, which the Lord our God hath commanded you?" (KJV) Verse 21 carries on with an example of how to testify to your child of the world; of God in your experience.

Prayer Log

Keep a special diary of the child's special prayer requests. Enter the prayer and dates asked on the left side of the page, and leave the right half blank to record God's answer when it comes. You might want to include a note on a lesson learned or an unexpected benefit gained when God did not answer positively.

Name Projects

It has been pointed out that people tend to live up to the meaning of their names. For this reason, it is important that parents know the meanings of the names of their children and work to attach special literal, biblical, and character connotations to them. Here are some ways to do that:

Name Plaques

Make or buy a plaque. For a motif, you may be able to find a card of the child's name

at the Christian book store. Otherwise, you may want to make up your own paper with the child's name printed, drawn, or written in calligraphy on it. We've found some pieces at a Christian book shop with the child's name in large bold print and the meaning underneath. If you make your own—or better yet, let the child make his own—be sure to include a Bible verse with some reference to a character quality reflected in the meaning of the name. Finish the plaque, after gluing the paper down, according to the directions on your favorite decoupage lacquer.

Name Seats

If you have a woodworker in the family, you may want to replace your dining room chairs with some homemade benches. You can personalize the benches by applying a printing of each child's name at his place. You could apply a paper with the name on it, or perhaps imprint the name and meaning on the bench by means of wood burning or staining. If paper is used, once again you will need to apply decoupage material as a cover.

102

Name Plates

This is a great gift idea for Christmas.

A unique way to remind your son or daughter of the meaning of his or her name is by means of personalized name plates.

Send $3.95 to this address: SMALL FRY ORIGINALS, Plastics Manufacturing Co., P.O. Box 24645, Dallas, TX 75224-0445. They will send you a kit that is an excellent value. It contains a set of 12 very good markers and 50 mats that serve as patterns for the plates. Let the child draw a picture or write a Bible verse on the mat, along with his name and its meaning. Then send the completed mat back to the same address along with $2.00 for each plate. By the way, they can only make one plate from each mat. We received our plates back in about 10 days. The company includes little wire hooks you can use to hang the plates on the wall if you choose not to use them for dining. We eat on ours. This is one of the best projects we have found as far as value received for dollar spent. The plates are white in background, Melamine, and dishwasher safe.

Name Songs

Our friend Jana Getz is in Heaven now, but she left many children with a legacy in the form of Scripture songs. She had at least one book of songs published and when she taught in the Christian school where we used to go to church, she composed a Scripture song reflecting the meaning of the name of each of the twenty- or thirty-some kids who attended there. Many of you will have musical ability enough to compose a simple little jingle for your child's name using a Bible verse or idea. You may find one, as we did for Timothy (honoring God) on a children's record. One way to use the songs is to have a music time each day to sing these songs, hymns, and others. By the way, an autoharp is an excellent investment for a family, especially if you have no piano. Anyone can learn to play one well, and it gives a pretty and versatile sound.

Name Dolls

I use a sheet or scrap fabric cut into the shape of a small doll. Before you assemble the

cut pieces of the doll, let the kids color the front with Vogart liquid embroidery paints, available at department stores. They come in a tube, are neat and manageable even for small children, and and long lasting. Draw a big heart on the chest. We wrote the meaning of the name and underlined it at the top of the chest. On Timmy's doll for example, we wrote, "My name is Timmy, to remind me that God's purpose for my life is to live as a shining example for God so that the world will see how great God is, and they will want to honor God with their lives too." Rickey's says, Brave, Powerful Ruler (name meaning) and "My name is Rickey because God wants to teach me how to let His power flow through me in order to lead others to a knowledge of Him. He also wants to teach me to be a good leader by first being a servant."

Place Mats

Marilyn sewed heavy clear plastic together to make a cover for place mats. The plastic is sewn on 3 sides only, to allow for removal and replacement of the mat itself. The mats are drawn by the kids themselves on light colored construction paper. At the top, Joshua's mat says, "God Made Me in a Special Way for a Special Purpose." Below that, in letters large enough to take up about a third of the height of the paper, "JOSHUA." Below the name, "God is my salvation," his name's meaning, in much smaller letters, and another color. Below that, in normal size handwriting "My name is Joshua. Joshua means, 'God is my salvation.' This reminds me that only God can save me from my sin and only God can protect me. It also reminds me to share with others that God can save them too." Then, below that in the left corner, "Bible Example— Paul." On the back, in print big enough to take up the bulk of the page, let the kids write a Bible verse. We used verses from Psalm 139 as our goal was to teach self-acceptance, which is an excellent chapter in that regard.

Paper Kid

Have the child lie down on a large piece of paper, such as you might find sold in rolls. Trace the outline of the child's body with a

marker. Let the child write his name on the paper, along with a message about the child's name. For Katie we wrote "My name is Katie. It means, 'Pure,' to remind me that if I am pure on the inside, then I can understand and know God in a very special way."

Miscellaneous Projects

With fabric crayons or tube paints, write the child's name and its meaning on pillow shams, quilts, or bedroom curtains. Cross-stitch names and meanings. Let the child make clay or papier mâché models of his name. Plant the name in seeds and watch it grow. Make beads of modeling clay, string them with needle and thread, write on each a letter of the name, and let them dry for a little girl's necklace.

Meaning of a Name

An excellent book to help track down the meanings of names is *What's in a Name* by Linda Francis, John Hartzell and As Palmquist.

FUN PROJECTS
for **Hands–On Character Building** ....
Section 4
Building Self-Acceptance

107

It is published by Ark Products, Minneapolis, MN 55420. The format is really neat.

Example:

- Name: **FLORA**

- Literal Meaning: **A FLOWER**

- Suggested Character Quality or Godly Characteristic: **FRAGRANT SPIRIT**

- Suggested Lifetime Scripture Verse—II Corinthians 2:14: **"But thanks be to God, Who invariably leads us on triumphantly in Christ and evidences through us in every place the fragrance that results from knowing him."**

We think this book is really great. Many of our friends have used it to investigate the names they were interested in before the birth of the new baby.

Good Thing Tell

Go around the table at dinner or the living room at devotions time. Dad or Mom says,

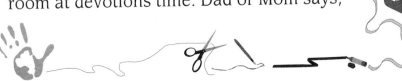

"Everyone tell me one good thing about Nathan." Then the same for each other family member. It might be good to include a friend or other relative occasionally, too.

Monthly Special Night Out

Once each month, take a different child out for lunch or supper with Mom and Dad. Let him choose the place, the meal, and the topic of conservation. Use every opportunity to say something positive about the child and tell him how special he is to you. Try, in a relaxed way, to help him talk about the things he thinks and feels and is interested in. Remember, the purpose of the occasion is to make him feel special.

Framed Verses

Let each child write and illustrate a Bible verse. Put the works of art in good picture frames and hang them in conspicuous places throughout the house. This lets him know you

like his work and assume that others will want
to see it, too.

Quality Consciousness

Jump on every opportunity to praise
examples of character qualities as the child
demonstrates them. Example: "Oh, Daddy!
Did you see what Matthew did? He picked
up his shoes without being told, and put them
in his closet! What initiative!" The younger
the child is, the more you can ham it up
without seeming insincere. Remember to
name the quality. This teaches the child to be
quality-conscious. Some parents would be
amazed, should they try this, to see how much
better behavior results from this approach than
from constantly reminding Junior when he
is doing the wrong thing.

Spontaneous Huggery

At least once per day, out of the blue, call
the child to you and surprise him with a big
hug. Hold him on your lap just a minute (if he

will fit) and tell him he is special, you love him, and you are glad God gave him to you. This is perhaps best done when not immediately preceded by any special positive behavior on his part; it reminds him you love him not because of what he does, but just because of who he is.

Spiritual Journal/Scrapbook

Help Junior keep a diary of important spiritual events in his life. Salvation, baptism, an occasion of asking someone's forgiveness, a memorized verse or chapter of Scripture, insights from Scripture, etc.

Self-Image Lunch

Illustrate the fact that we have value as we are, but God is not finished with us yet. Serve lunch with all or several of the menu items lacking one ingredient. For example, bread without butter, herb tea without honey, sandwiches without mayonnaise, salad without dressing, cake without frosting.

Daily "Special Time"

111

After lunch, Marilyn reads a spiritual story to the kids together. She may use *Character Sketches, Child's Guide to Character Building*, or a chapter from the life story of a famous Christian. Then she sends them off to naps. She keeps one child with her as the others go off to bed and reads another story to him, chats with him, sends him to nap time, and then calls another for his special time. Doing it one child at a time makes it more special.

Personalized Songs

When singing together as a family or just with a child or children, replace words in the song where appropriate with the child's name and proper pronouns, etc. Example: "Jesus loves Rickey, this he knows, for the Bible tells Rickey so. Little Rickey to Him belongs, Rickey is weak but He is strong. Yes, Jesus loves Rickey..."

112

Rickey's Baby

The purpose of this project is twofold: First, it reassures the first (or second, third, or whatever) child that he is special, regardless of how many other children are in the family. Secondly, it conditions the older child to understand that the new baby is special in its own way, helping to avoid the possibility that the older child will treat the younger child less than kindly after it arrives, seeing it as a competitor rather than a compatriot. When the new baby is still inside Mommy, tell the next older sibling that God is going to give him (not Mommy and Daddy) a new baby of his very own. Mommy will have to do much of the work, but big brother will get to help Mommy take care of Baby: feeding it, washing it, cleaning up after it, etc. Every day up to delivery, remind him how special he must be to God, because God is giving him his very own baby. Help him make a gift for the new baby before it arrives, let him help decorate the nursery, let him write to Grandma (whether Grandma can read his "writing," or not) telling her how excited he is about his baby, etc. We have done things of this sort with each of our six "big brother and sisters" and we have never had any appreciable problem with jealousy toward the new baby.

Hand and Footprints

Mix plaster of Paris according to the directions on the package. If it seems too runny, add more powder. Press the child's hand or foot into the mix, which needs only to be mounted on a piece of plywood or newspaper. Press a paper clip into the back while still moist to make a hanger. After drying, write with a marker, "Fearfully and wonderfully made" or some such message on the cast, and do not forget to scratch the date into it before the mix hardens too much. These can be adapted to make nice presents for grandparents, serving as a yearly Christmas reminder of another year's growth. This project also serves to remind the kids of their individuality, and the fact that they are God's developing—not-finished—project.

114

Work

The earliest means of motivation a parent can use on his child is doing the job with him.

One of the most important and most neglected things God has designed to give us a feeling of purpose and importance as children is work. Certainly many people have never given serious thought to work as a character builder, and probably more than a few of us were victims of parents who tried to motivate us to work by strictly negative means, leaving us with a negative attitude toward any job that is not strictly our own idea. Certain basics need to be in place for children to develop a proper attitude toward work. The earliest means of motivation a parent can use on his child is doing the job with him. The temptation is to leave the child alone to do his work as soon as he is competent to perform it alone, but this immediately destroys a large part of Junior's reason for wanting to do the job: a desire to be with Mom or Dad. The more you cheerfully work with the child, the more cheerfully he will work both in the earlier and later years. It is no less than a crime against our children to neglect to teach them to work, and it is little better to teach them—by making them work alone—that work is boring drudgery.

Another important motivation is simple appreciation. Some parents can get their kids to obey and work, but fail to express generous appreciation for the job done. One of the surest ways to demotivate anybody from working for you is to act as if whatever they did was no more than you had a right to expect, and probably not as much.

Why is work a self-image builder? It shows the child that he is competent—that he can learn to do something important, just like the big people. It teaches him that he is important, that Mommy needs his help. It makes the child feel, if properly directed, that he is a part of a team; he belongs and has a role to play for which he was specially chosen by God.

Our kids, the oldest of whom is 19 at this writing, do all the vacuuming and dusting in our home. They do the sweeping, mopping, laundry, and wall washing almost entirely. They help in the garden, tilling and weeding, as well

as the fun stuff, such as planting. Furthermore, they help pick and can or freeze the produce. In the past 3 years, I have probably spent less than 5 hours mowing our 1/2-acre lawn. The boys do that too. Sure, our kids gripe sometimes. They have too much of their father's blood in them to do otherwise. But they do their work mostly with a positive attitude and would do even better if we would put forth a little more effort to train them properly.

Baby Bedtime Routine

When Emily was our youngest, Marilyn put her to bed each night, using a process you may find helpful. She has used basically the same approach with each of our babies, and I think it is great. First, she carries Baby around the room, talking to her just as if she understood perfectly every word. "Look, Emmy, there's your name plaque. It says that your name means 'diligent.' And look here on Katie's bedspread, Emmy. Here's a picture of Emmy taking care of Mattie when he's sick. Emmy is being compassionate to Mattie. And here's Katie in this picture rocking Emmy. Katie is being gentle

to Emmy." And so on. Then Marilyn sings to Emmy, a little song written by Jana Getz, paraphrased to personalize it for Emmy:

Thank You God that You made me (Emmy)

Just the way I am (she is)

Thank You God that You made me (Emmy)

According to Your plan.

Thank You God that You loved me (Emmy)

Enough to give Your Son for me (Emmy)

Thank You God that You made me (Emmy)

Just the way I am (she is)

Then Marilyn puts Baby in her bed and prays with her, asking God to bless Emmy and help Mommy and Daddy to train Emmy to want to serve God more than anything else in the world. Finally, Mommy turns on Katie and Emmy's bedtime tape. This is a cassette recording of Daddy reading a Bible story to the girls, preceded by a personalized introduction from Daddy to daughters. As Mom leaves the room and turns down the dimmer switch, she says goodnight to the baby

118

and reminds her that Mommy loves her. Usually Emily goes to sleep immediately so that those words are the last she hears.

I Am Special

This is another song Jana Getz wrote to teach children that they are special to God. We have sung it with our children for years. Sing it to the tune of Jesus Loves Me:

I am special, this I know,

For the Bible tells me so.

God knew me before my birth

And planned each day of my life on earth.

Chorus:

Yes, Jesus made me,

Yes, Jesus made me,

Yes, Jesus made me,

I am wonderfully made.

I am fashioned by God's hand

Unto good works throughout the land

For in Him I'll learn to be

All He's prepared especially for me.

Even though I make mistakes

God forgives for His name's sake

He helps me to be kind and good

And do the things I know I should.

I am precious in God's sight

And in Him my soul delights

He loves me and died for me

That I might live eternally.

Taping Day
Tape your children talking and or singing.

Once every several months at least, especially on special days such as Christmas and other landmark dates, tape each of the children talking and or singing. Whenever we replay one of the tapes from our children's past, each child just lights up whenever he hears his own voice. It seems to make a child

feel extra special for his parents to value him enough to want to preserve his childhood on tape. They love to listen to themselves as they sounded when they were "little."

Family "Paper" Dolls

Our little girls love paper dolls. But after having bought umpteen sets of the cut-out dolls offered in the stores, we finally came up with an idea to provide the same fun in a more durable form. Cut the picture of a family member out of a 5x7 color enlargement. Glue it on a piece of 1/4-inch long plywood. Use a jigsaw to cut the plywood around the edge of the photo figure. You now have a "paper" doll in the shape of a family member and with that person's picture on it. Finish it with 3 coats of Mod podge. We made little stands from small blocks of 3/4-inch pine by sawing a 1/4-inch-wide slot in the top of the block and gluing the bottom of the paper doll into the slot so it would stand up. The little girls were using their paper dolls to play-act family situations and now they have look-alike family dolls to do it with.

Refrigerator Magnet Pictures

121

Again, glue a picture of a family member on plywood. Cut an oval or circle out of the plywood, finish with 3 coats of Mod podge, and sand the edges of the plywood for smoothness. Glue a magnetic strip on the back.

Hand Print T-Shirts

Using acrylic paints, paint the child's hands. Place his hands on a t-shirt and press down. Paint on the child's name and its meaning, and add a Bible verse with an appropriate thought.

Family Baby Rattle

This is a commercial product sold by "The First Years" company. It consists of a thick plastic ring like a big key ring holding flat, slotted cases into which you can slip pictures of family members.

Section 5
Building A
Forgiving Spirit

*For if you forgive men
for their transgressions,
your heavenly Father
will also forgive you.*

MATTHEW 6:14 NASB

Section 5
Building A Forgiving Spirit

124

J ESUS TAUGHT HIS *disciples to pray to be forgiven as they themselves forgave those who trespassed against them.*

If it is important to be forgiven, it is also important to forgive.

Forgiving is one of the hardest things to do. Others can, often without meaning to do so, do and say things that wound us deeply. But to fail to forgive is to deny healing to yourself as well as the offender. He who fails to forgive must live with the destructive forces of bitterness within, and is much more to be pitied than the one who offended. Bitterness is like a cancer and can in fact cause a number of physical ailments—due to the body's constant production of strong chemicals in response to what the brain tells it is an unresolved conflict. Even worse, the root of bitterness can spring up and defile or infect many others. A hurt that was once between two people can become an infectious disease that, if untreated, will leave permanent scars on the lives of others. One needs only to look

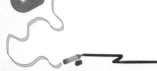

as far as a family member who has suffered the pain of divorce for an example.

We must forgive our children when they do wrong, even if they must still be punished. We must ask forgiveness of them when we are wrong, if we are to teach them to clear their consciences and keep conflicts resolved. In addition, we must be alert to potential offenses between family members and head off problems before they erupt.

FUN PROJECTS

Investing Treasure

If a child has a problem with another child in the family or the neighborhood, develop a project for him to give a gift or do something kind for the other child. A gift in secret pacifies anger.

126 Hug Therapy

If a child wrongs another child in the family, have him ask forgiveness and give the other a hug. Physical contact is very important in the family.

Asking Forgiveness

It is very important that children learn early to take responsibility for their words and actions toward others. For that reason, when your child wrongs someone—inside the family or out—guide him in asking forgiveness and making restitution if that is indicated. One of our girls misbehaved for a baby-sitter once, and we made her call the next day and ask the baby-sitter for forgiveness. The sitter later told us it was very touching to her.

Good Report

When your child speaks negatively of another person, have him list verbally three good things about that person.

Matthew 5:44

"But I say to you, love your enemies, and pray for those who persecute you."

God gives here a project for dealing with those who irritate us. He is quite specific:

Action	Reaction
An enemy (opponent)	Love him
One who curses me	Bless him (speak well)
One who hates me	Do good to him
One who spitefully uses me (slander, etc.)	Pray for him

Thought Patterns

When a child has a bad attitude toward another, discuss Philippians 4:8 with him and talk about how he can think about the person in these ways.

Section 6
Building Meekness

*But the meek
shall inherit the earth;
and shall delight themselves
in the abundance of peace.*

—*PSALM 37:11 KJV*

130

BLESSED, THE BIBLE SAYS, *are the meek. They shall inherit the earth. Meekness could be translated "gentleness," and often is in modern versions of Scripture.*

True meekness is not weakness, as in a person who has no convictions and just lets the world go by without ever causing any ripples. It involves a sense of the justice and mercy of God, the ability to see beyond the immediate to the permanent and eternal. A meek person is the only person who can have real peace. He has surrendered his rights to Christ, realizing that He has bought and paid for those rights with His own blood. This spirit of gentleness requires a submission to God, taking rightful responsibility but trusting Him for results beyond our control. It means recognizing that Jesus is Lord over all my life, that I belong to Him and it is His responsibility to do in my life what is right.

Meekness is the key to receiving the grace from God, for He resists the proud but gives grace to the humble. Meekness is also the key to serving others, for unless we have

FUN PROJECTS
for **Hands–On Character Building**
....

Section 6
Building Meekness

131

given ourselves and our rights to God, we still have the need to protect them and must therefore look; to protecting our rights rather than meeting the needs of others.

FUN PROJECTS

Rickey Board

Have the child lie down on a sheet of plywood. Trace around the outline of his body with a felt-tip marker. Outline on the resulting picture the facial features, hair and clothes. Let the child color in the figure, but do any fine-detail work that is beyond your child's capabilities. Use a large enough piece of plywood so that you have 6 to 8 inches of space around the figure to write on. Above the figure, write Romans 12:1. Write the entire verse out, not just the reference. Then go down the board on all sides of the figure, writing in verses that apply to parts of the body at the level of the body where the body part appears, or nearby with an arrow from the verse to the part. Go over the board with the child occasionally, discussing the meaning of surrendering the various body parts to God. Check

several different versions of Scripture for the best rendering of each verse for your child's understanding. Because we drew Rickey wearing overalls, I Peter 5:5 was excellent in the Phillips' version. In each verse, underline the name of the body part it mentions.

Part of Body	Scripture Verse
Hair	Matthew 10:30
Ears, head, neck	Proverbs 1:8–9
Eyes	Proverbs 4:25
Ears	Proverbs 4:20
Lips	Proverbs 8:6, 21:23
Neck	Proverbs 3:3
Hands	Proverbs 10:4
Fingers, heart	Proverbs 7:3
Loins	Ephesians 6:14
Knees	Ephesians 3:14
Feet	Proverbs 4:27, Ephesians 6:15

Quiet Time

Teach your child to give up his own right to speak and act as he chooses by using this exercise to develop his self-control. This, incidentally, is an excellent training for "hyperactive" kids. We often call a quiet time when we, the parents need to talk or we are driving in the car and things have gotten a bit too rowdy for proper concentration. It is obviously a benefit for the parents, but even more for the children. It doesn't come naturally for a child to sit and be still, and this is further aggravated in our society by sugar-rich diets, fast-paced lifestyles, and in many misled families, television. You can take a very active child such as our Rickey was, and train him to be quiet in spirit and under real self-control by helping him master this skill of being quiet.

To start with, it may be necessary to utilize some sanctified bribery. Promise Junior some of his favorite treat if he can sit absolutely still, moving nothing except to blink, for 30 seconds. Some kids actually cannot do that, and you will have to repeat the exercise a few times before he makes it to the 30-

second mark. Of course, you will want to do this at a quiet moment in the home with a minimum of distractions to start. Once Junior's tolerance level has built up to the 30-second level, try a minute. Increase the time by small increments until he can sit still as a statue for 10 minutes. This project should be done over a period of several days or weeks, and the training sessions should be kept as short as needed, depending on the child's present tolerance level. If this project sounds too simple to work, let me assure you that it works as well as anything I have ever seen to calm a "hyperactive" child. One of the most hyperactive children I ever new was trained by his mother using this method. He went to kindergarten, and for months he kept the classroom in an uproar. His mother, under good counsel from a more experienced mother, began quiet time training. Before the year was over, the child's teacher told his mother that her son had become a joy to have in class. This, by the way, is an excellent training for 2-year-olds who need to learn to sit through family devotions.

Nathan Night

Nathan (or whoever) gets to have fun developing a servant's heart on this special night. Nathan plans for, shops for, cooks and serves a meal, and chooses one to pick the menu from among the other boys and girls in the family. He does not choose the items himself, but gets to feel special serving the others.

For Guest Night, the kids team up together to serve others. Perhaps they get to choose whom to invite over; it should be someone really special or someone with a special need. The children work together to plan, shop for, cook, and serve the meal.

Meekness Flash Cards

Among your character flash cards, there should be one with, on one side, the reference Matthew 5:5 and a smiling face. On the other side, write, "Rickey believes that whatever Mommy and Daddy tell him is the very best thing for him right now." Apparently, kids can

136

really internalize this principle. When Rickey was 2- or 3-years-old, we drove past a McDonald's restaurant where the Ronald McDonald statue out front had been knocked down by a car. When he saw it, Rickey noted Ronald's smiling face and said very excitedly, " Mommy, look! Ronald the Donald fell down and he's still meek!"

Service Projects

Have the kids organize special efforts to serve others, especially those in spiritual authority over them, older relatives, and those who have special needs, e.g. widows, old people, poor people, hospital and nursing home patients, etc. What can little kids do to serve? With a little help from parents, they can wash windows, cut grass, trim hedges, wash cars, take meals, walk dogs, clean houses, weed gardens, make gifts, draw greeting cards, read Scripture, sing or play instruments, etc. We once got our pastor's approval to take the tithe of our garden produce to a widow in our church.

Museum Ministry

Our kids came up with this idea on their own. Collect a home "museum" of interesting or unusual artifacts. Fortunately for the budding young curators, most of their clientele will be children and sympathetic adults, so it does not really have to compete with the Smithsonian. Sea shells collected last summer, a snakeskin, new puppies, and a host of other homely oddities can serve as specimens. Invite friends to come on a certain day or even on an open schedule and view the exhibits. Let the kids serve punch and cookies, etc. For unsaved neighborhood friends, Gospel tracts may be in order; Bible story comic books, if you can find them, may be even better.

Meek Puppets

Have the children draw a picture of themselves on a brown lunch bag and make a meek (smiling in spite of adversity) face. We always talk about having corners up, meaning corners of the mouth. You can invent all kinds of adversity stories and all kinds of lessons the puppet children learned through their hard times. The puppets are very talented; in fact, they can even act out Bible stories such as Noah (publicly mocked), Elijah (hunted by wicked Jezebel), or Paul (stoned, beaten, shipwrecked).

Nap time

Everyone needs to develop a disciplined period of time each day to give attention to God's Word. We use nap time each afternoon for this purpose. While the babies nap, the older children read an assigned number of Bible chapters, do their verse memorization assignments, etc. This is also a good time, along with night bedtime, to play Scripture cassette tapes. All this is done in their bedrooms. The older kids are not required to sleep, but they are to stay on their beds and be quiet, reading or memorizing or listening to the tapes. We will explain more about the Bible tapes, a very valuable tool, later.

Traffic Light Word Check

139

Here is a fun learning game for children in the younger years.

On your bulletin board, cover the face of the board with paper. On the paper, draw a landscape—Mommy and kids together, of course—and include a roadway in the middle. Have a starting line drawn on the "map" and a destination at the other end. At the starting point, line up several construction paper car shapes pointing down the road. On the visible side of each car, write the reference to a Scripture verse, and on the back side, the verse itself. For example, on the front write Proverbs 16:24, on the back, "Pleasant words are as an honeycomb, sweet to the soul, and health to the bones." Use different colors of construction paper to make the scene as appealing as possible to small children

Once you have your scene constructed and your cars tacked in place, make a big to-do of placing a construction paper traffic light on the road near the starting point. Beside the intersection, draw in a parking lot. Beside

140

the parking lot, erect a sign reading, "DEAD END WORDS PARK HERE".

Have each child in turn take a car, unpin it, and move it ahead to the traffic light. If he chose a car that bore a verse on the back dealing with a negative kind of words, have him drive it into the dead end parking lot. If he chose a car with a verse about positive words, let him drive on to the destination. The end of the game is to get the good word cars to the end of the journey and all the bad word cars into the dead end parking lot. While the process is going on, talk to the kids about the kinds of words the cars represent. Discuss what might be examples of each kind of words.

Head-to-Foot Construction Paper Dolls

Marilyn drew a basic form of a child on a big sheet of construction paper. Then she cut out overalls, shirts, hands, hair, lips, feet, eyes, legs, etc. On each garment or body part, she wrote Bible verses about how we should use all the parts of our body for God The

children pasted parts to the basic form and Marilyn talked with them about each part as they did it. This project, of course, was developed with younger children in mind, but would be a good learning opportunity for older kids if they were given the job of "administering" the game with the little ones.

Gripe Stopper

When a child complains about doing household chores, bookwork or whatever, require him to quote Philippians 2:14 "Be glad you can do the things you should be doing. Do all things without arguing, and talking about how you wish you did not have to do them " For general-purpose complaining, make the child tell you three things he is thankful for.

Drawer Check

Ever have a problem getting the kids to keep their dresser drawers neat and orderly? Here is a fun project that really works. Announce early in the week that on Friday

142

Mom is going to check all drawers and there will be a treat for those who have kept their drawers neat. Sometimes all the kids will run off and straighten up their drawers immediately, with the expected result that they are a disaster again by Friday, probably several times over. But remind them again on Thursday evening and most of them will look pretty good on Friday. Leave a small treat of candy, gum, or a small toy in each neat drawer. Do not be too strict, but do not be too lenient, either. Just make sure the kids have notice in advance but not too far in advance, and repeat it as often as you feel necessary the first few times you try it. Gradually reduce the number of warnings over the weeks and begin to hold spot checks without notice except that there will be an unannounced drawer check soon. The goal is to work your way to the point where the drawers will be kept neat at all times. We eventually began to do room checks, too.

FUN PROJECTS
for **Hands–On Character Building**
....
Section 6
Building Meekness

143

Section 7
Building A
Strong Testimony

*You are the light
of the world.
A city set on a hill
cannot be hidden.*

—MATTHEW 5:14 NASB

146

ATTHEW CHAPTER 5, in verses 10 through 12, tells us that we should rejoice in being persecuted and reviled for the sake of righteousness.

The quality of being willing to take a stand for that which is right is an important quality to learn. If our children do not see their parents take a stand on that which is absolutely right and that which is absolutely wrong, they will find it hard to learn themselves. In addition, they need to be taught and encouraged to find ways to make a humble but confident testimony for the Lord Jesus Christ.

The following projects can be used to guide your children in creatively testifying to your family's faith.

Fabric Crayon T-Shirts
Make the Word of God a part of our wearing apparel.

Earlier in the book we talked about how to make these shirts; here is one way in which

FUN PROJECTS
for **Hands–On Character Building**
....

Section 7
Building A Strong Testimony

147

to use them. Deuteronomy 6:8 exhorts us to make the Word of God a part of our wearing apparel. Part of the reason this is a good idea is that it is a bold testimony to the world. Everyone recognizes a product by its label. There is an element of identification in the wrapper in which we enclose God's product, too. When we put the Scriptures on garments we are saying to all the world, "I am glad to belong to Jesus Christ. He is the King of the universe, and I do not apologize for or hide the fact that I belong to Him."

FUN PROJECTS

Neighborhood Ministry

First, a caution. Most children, in fact nearly all of them, spend far too much time with kids their own age. This is the biggest factor in their tendency to grow disrespectful toward their parents' counsel and develop an attitude of contempt toward their younger siblings. Any time you encourage them to spend ministering to the neighborhood

148

youngsters should be carefully weighed against the ballast of their priorities.

That done, however, your kids can really let their lights shine with just a little help from you. If your kids are decent, friendly, controlled kids who have never developed the common hypercompetitive spirit of kids today, your home may be so popular as a playground that it becomes a problem. In addition to being a place where kids can play without pressure and competition, your home can also be used creatively to be even more attractive to your children's friends.

Some of the things our kids have planned for their friends include a picnic to which each child was assigned to bring one food item, plays based on Bible stories and in which each of the neighbor kids played a part, T-shirt making sessions, Christmas cookie (manger scene) parties where the kids bake together, etc. A variation of the manger scene idea is to make a manger scene by sticking the cookies down on foil wrapped cardboard and then deliver the sets to friends or neighbors.

Exercising Discernment

Your child will occasionally have the opportunity to make use of his growing ability to discern between that which is right and that which is wrong or questionable. Years ago we attended a church that emphasized children's ministries and featured, among other things, movies for the children at times during which the adults were involved in special programs such as concerts, banquets, etc. On a couple of occasions our kids, under the leadership of our oldest son, got up and walked out of the activity. On one such occasion, a young lady who was serving as a supervisor for the children told the kids that they could not leave. Little Rickey then explained to her that his Mom and Dad had objections to certain kinds of fantasy and other such things, and that he knew they would not be comfortable with their children sitting through such an activity. Apparently she was convinced. She capitulated and Rickey baby-sat his siblings for the remainder of the evening in another room.

150

Children who have a healthy self-image resulting from plenty of parental love and internalization of Scripture will be surprisingly free from peer pressure and willing to take a stand on that which is right. They will also tend to notice and be upset by the things other children do that are wrong, even if they themselves are not the objects of the wrong action or attitude. They need parents who will encourage them to be alert to wrong (rare people) and who will also be diligent and watchful to teach the children to hate sin while still loving the sinner.

Testimony by Mail

Our kids occasionally write to government officials and other people in positions of authority. One of them once wrote to the governor and enclosed a Gospel tract. Another letter went to the office of a shopping mall near us, asking that a manger scene be included in the mall's Christmas decorations. Kids could also write to managers of stores, asking them to stop selling liquor or pornography. They could write to town

officials, such as those in one Virginia city that considers spanking to be child abuse and requires medical personnel by law to report marks on a child's body that indicate the child has been spanked. The latter example may not turn out to be the most popular topic of kids' appeal letters.

If's

This has been discussed earlier, but deserves repetition here as a method of teaching a child to take a stand. For instance: "Timmy, you're at a friend's house and he says, 'Let's watch TV, Tim. This is a good show. Your Dad would not mind!' What do you say to him?"

Conclusion
A Few Words...

154

few things need to be mentioned in conclusion. First, the projects in this book were created and collected over 19 years of parenthood. Do not make the mistake of trying to use them all in one year. Select a few that really appeal to you and use them with your children. Do not try to do everything at once. Why make it complicated?

Secondly, you may have noticed that many of these projects are generally oriented toward young children as opposed to adolescents. When we are asked what to do for older kids, we suggest among other things that the older siblings in the family help the younger ones with these projects. This builds the relationship between the older and younger children, and reinforces the concepts in the minds of the older ones.

Personal Note

We thought you might like to hear what one of our own children has to say after having worked through many of these projects over a period of several years. So we asked our

eldest, Richard (age 19), to write a few lines
to help us conclude. Here is his message:

"A quick note of corroboration, just to show that
the ones most affected by these projects still
remember them and that they really do work. The
one I remember best is probably the 'Ifs'. Mom
used to do those with us, it seemed like most
every day, and almost every time I would stop to
consider what I was about to do I would think, 'If
this happened, what would you do?' It was more
often than not the stop sign I needed.

The Character Sketch Quilts were probably
Mom's best investment of time out of all the
projects. I only abandoned mine a couple of years
ago, because the poor thing was 12 or 15 years
old and sadly thread bare. I still have it in the
closet, of course, and still occasionally stop
and mentally thank Mom for her investment of time
and character for me.

For you hassled moms, too, I can't say enough
about 'Training Sessions' in the supermarket. Of
course in our case, there was always some doubt
as to whether we were more out of the way in
a straight line or in a tight group. I never really got
into the habit of reaching for things from the
shelves or repeating, 'Mom, let's get this, Mom,

156

let's get that.' With Dad acting as traffic policeman, Mom was able to get her shopping done with much less trouble, until eventually it was just habit and Dad didn't have to be there to protect the store's property.

I could say more about most of these ideas, but I will just say one more thing: Thanks, Mom and Dad."